GIBRALTAR
0°
• Ceuta
• Tangier

M E D I T E R R A N E A N   S E A

TUNISIA

ALGERIA

LIBYA

EGYPT

20°

RED SEA

S   A   H   A   R   A

20°

Timbuktoo

MALI

NIGER

CHAD

SUDAN

Khartoum

Blue Nile
White Nile
Nile

L. TANA

DJIBOUTI

PER
LTA

Niger

GHANA
TOGO
BENIN

Kainji Reservoir
Kainji Dam

NIGERIA

CAMEROON

CENT.
AFRICAN REP

ETHIOPIA

SOMALIA

SLAVE COAST
COAST
BIGHT OF
BENIN
BIGHT OF
BIAFRA
FERNANDO PO
EQUATORIAL GUINEA
SÃO TOMÉ
CAPE ST. CATHERINE

GABON

Congo

Gondokoro

Juba

UGANDA

Kampala
× Kabaka's Court
L. VICTORIA

KENYA

0°

ZAIRE

Lualaba

CONGO BASIN

RWANDA

BURUNDI

• Tabora

• Mombasa

Brazzaville
• Kinshasa
CABINDA

L.
TANGANYIKA

Mpwapwa

ZANZIBAR

Bagamoyo

• Loanda

TANZANIA

ANGOLA

• Mikindani

Rovuma

• Benguela

CAPE ST. MARY

Area of large scale map

ZAMBIA

MALAWI

L.
NYASA

Shire

CAPE NEGRO

Seshecke

Zambezi

RHODESIA

MOZAMBIQUE

Quelimane

L.
NGAMI

SOUTH
WEST
AFRICA

CAPE CROSS

BOTSWANA

SWAZILAND

Kuruman

Alexander Bay

SOUTH
AFRICA

LESOTHO

CAPE COLONY

Cape Town
CAPE OF GOOD HOPE
Mossel Bay
• Port Elizabeth

A T L A N T I C   O C E A N

I N D I A N   O C E A N

20°

0°
20°
40°

J. P. Tremblay

The River Congo

Also by Peter Forbath

SEVEN SEASONS